WU WEI

WU WEI

A Phantasy Based on the Philosophy of Lao-Tse

HENRI BOREL

Published by
Rupa Publications India Pvt. Ltd 2017
7/16, Ansari Road, Daryaganj
New Delhi 110002

Sales centres:
Allahabad Bengaluru Chennai
Hyderabad Jaipur Kathmandu
Kolkata Mumbai

Copyright © Rupa Publications India Pvt. Ltd 2017

This is a work of fiction. Names, characters, places and incidents are either the product of the author's imagination or are used fictitiously and any resemblance to any actual person, living or dead, events or locales is entirely coincidental.All rights reserved.

No part of this publication may be reproduced, transmitted, or stored in a retrieval system, in any form or by any means, electronic, mechanical, photocopying, recording or otherwise, without the prior permission of the publisher.

ISBN: 978-81-291-4525-3

First impression 2017

10 9 8 7 6 5 4 3 2 1

Printed at Parksons Graphics Pvt. Ltd. Mumbai.

This book is sold subject to the condition that it shall not, by way of trade or otherwise, be lent, resold, hired out, or otherwise circulated, without the publisher's prior consent, in any form of binding or cover other than that in which it is published.

CONTENTS

PREFACE / vii
TAO / 1
ART / 29
LOVE / 59
NOTES / 85

PREFACE

The following study on Lao-Tse's 'Wu-Wei' should by no means be regarded as a translation or even as a free rendering of the actual work of that philosopher. I have simply endeavoured to retain in my work the pure essence of his thought, and I have given a direct translation of his essential truths in isolated instances only, the rest being for the most part a self-thought-out elaboration of the few principles enunciated by him.

My conception of the terms 'Tao' and 'WuWei' is entirely different from that of most sinologues (such as Stanislas Julien, Giles, and Legge), who have translated the work 'Tao-Teh-King.' But this is not the place to justify myself. It may best be judged from the following work whether my conception be reasonable or incorrect.

Little is contained in Lao-Tse's short, extremely simple book, the words of which may be said to be condensed into their purely primary significance—(a significance at times quite at variance with that given in other works to the same words*)—but this little is gospel. Lao-Tse's work is no treatise on philosophy, but contains, rather, merely those truths to which this (unwritten) philosophy had led him. In it we find no

---

*By Confucius, for instance.

PREFACE

form, nor embodiment, nothing but the quintessence of this philosophy.

My work is permeated with this essence, but it is no translation of Lao-Tse. None of my metaphorical comparisons, such as that with the landscape, with the sea, with the clouds, are anywhere to be found in Lao-Tse's work. Neither has he anywhere spoken of Art, nor specially of Love. In writing of all this I have spoken aloud the thoughts and feelings instinctively induced by the perusal of Lao-Tse's deep-felt philosophy. Thus it may be that my work contains far more of myself than I am conscious of; but even so, it is but an outpouring of the thought and feeling called up in me by the words of Lao-Tse.

I have made use of none but *Chinese* works on Lao-Tse, and of those, only a few. On reading later some of the English and French translations, I was amazed to find how confused and unintelligible these books were.

WU WEI

I adhered to my simple idea of Lao-Tse's work, and of my work I could alter nothing, for I felt the truth of it within me as a simple and natural faith.

Henri Borel

TAO

TAO

I was standing in the Temple of Shien Shan, on an islet in the Chinese Sea, distant a few hours' journey from the harbour of Ha Tó.

On either side rose mountain ranges, their soft outlines interwoven behind the island to the westward.

To the eastward shimmered the endless Ocean. High up, rock-supported, stood the Temple, in the shadow of broad Buddha-trees.

The island is but little visited, but sometimes fisher-folk, fleeing before the threatening typhoon, anchor there when they have no further hope of reaching the harbour. Why the Temple exists in this lonely spot, no one knows; but the lapse of centuries has established its holy right to stand there. Strangers arrive but seldom, and there are only a hundred poor inhabitants, or thereabouts, who live there simply because their ancestors did so before them. I had gone thither in the hope of finding some man of a serious bent of mind with whom to study. I had explored the temples and convents of the neighbourhood for more than a year, in search of earnest-minded priests capable of telling me what I was unable to learn from the superficial books on Chinese religion; but I found nothing but ignorant, stupid creatures everywhere—

kneeling to idols whose symbolical significance they did not understand, and reciting strange 'Sutras' not one word of which was intelligible to them.[1] And I had been obliged to draw all my information from badly translated works that had received even worse treatment at the hands of learned Europeans than at those of the literary Chinese whom I had consulted. At last, however, I had heard an old Chinaman speak of 'the Sage of Shien Shan' as of one well-versed in the secrets of Heaven and Earth; and—without cherishing any great expectations, it is true—I had crossed the water to seek him out.

This Temple resembled many others that I had seen. Grimy priests lounged on the steps in dirty-grey garments, and stared at me with senseless grins. The figures of 'Kwan Yin' and 'Cakyamuni' and, 'Sam-Pao-Fu' had been newly restored, and blazed with all imaginable crude colours that completely marred their former beauty. The floor was covered with dirt and dust, and pieces of orange peel and sugarcane were strewn about. A thick and heavy atmosphere oppressed my breast.

Addressing one of the priests, I said:

'I have come to visit the philosopher. Does not an old hermit dwell here, called after "Lao-Tse"?'

With a wondering face he answered me:

'Lao-Tse lives in the top-most hut upon the cliffs. But he does not like barbarians.'

I asked him quietly:

'Will you take me to him, Bikshu, for a dollar?'

There was greed in his glance, but he shook his head, saying:

'I dare not; seek him yourself.'

The other priests grinned, and offered me tea, in the hope of tips.

I left them, and climbed the rocks, reaching the top in half an hour; and there I found a little square stone hut. I knocked at the door, and, shortly after, heard some one draw back a bolt.

There stood the sage, looking at me.

And it was a revelation.

It seemed as though I saw a great light—a light not dazzling, but calming.

He stood before me tall and straight as a palm tree. His countenance was peaceful as is a calm evening, in the hush of the trees and the still moonlight; his whole person breathed the majesty of Nature, as simply beautiful, as purely spontaneous, as a mountain or a cloud. His presence radiated an atmosphere as holy as the prayerful soul in the soft after-gleam on a twilit landscape. As I felt uneasy under his deep gaze, and saw my poor life revealed in all its pettiness. I could not speak a word, but felt in silence his enlightening influence.

He raised his hand with a gesture like the movement of a swaying flower, and held it out to me heartily; frankly. He spoke, and his voice was soft music, like the sound of the wind in the trees:

'Welcome, stranger! What do you seek of me? Old man that I am!'

'I come to seek a master,' I answered humbly; 'to find the path to human goodness. I have long searched this beautiful land, but the people seem as though they were dead, and I am as poor as ever.'

'You err somewhat in this matter,' said the sage. 'Strive not so busily to be so very good. Do not seek it overmuch, or you will never find the true wisdom. Do you not know how it was that the Yellow Emperor'[2] recovered his magic pearl? I will tell you.[3]

'The Yellow Emperor once travelled round the north of the Red Sea, and climbed to the summit of the Kuenlun mountains. On his return to the southward, he lost his magic pearl. He besought his wits to find it, but in vain. He besought his sight to find it, but in vain. He besought his eloquence to find it, but that was also in vain. At last he besought Nothing, and

Nothing recovered it. "How extraordinary!" exclaimed the Yellow Emperor, "that Nothing should be able to recover it!" Do you understand me, young man?'

'I think this pearl was his soul,' I answered, 'and that knowledge, sight, and speech do but cloud the soul rather than enlighten it; and that it was only in the peace of perfect quietude that his soul's consciousness was restored to the Yellow Emperor. Is it so, Master?'

'Quite right; you have felt it as it is. And do you know, too, by whom this beautiful legend is told?'

'I am young and ignorant; I do not know.'

'It is by Chuang-Tse, the disciple of Lao-Tse, China's greatest philosopher. It was neither Confucius nor Mencius who spoke the purest wisdom in this country, but Lao-Tse. He was the greatest, and Chuang-Tse was his apostle. You foreigners cherish, I know, a certain well-meaning admiration for Lao-Tse also, but I think but few of you know that he was the purest human being who ever breathed. Have you read the "Tao-Teh-King"? and have you ever considered, I wonder, what he meant by "Tao"?'

'I should be grateful if you would tell me, Master.'

'I think I may well instruct you, young man. It is many years since I have had a pupil, and I see in your eyes no curiosity, but rather a pure desire for wisdom; for the freeing of your soul. Listen then—

'Tao is really nothing but that which you Westerners call "God". Tao is the One; the beginning and the end. It embraces all things, and to it all things return.

'Lao-Tse wrote at the commencement of his book the sign: Tao. But what he actually meant—the Highest, the One—can have no name, can never be expressed in any sound, just because it is The One. Equally inadequate is your term "God".—Wu—Nothing—that is Tao. You do not understand me?—Listen further! There exists, then, an absolute Reality—without beginning, without end—which we cannot comprehend, and which therefore must be to us as Nothing. That which we *are* able to comprehend, which has for us a relative reality, is in truth only appearance. It is an outgrowth, a result of absolute reality, seeing that everything emanates from, and returns to, that reality. But things which are real to us are not real in themselves. What we call Being is in fact Not-Being, and just what we call Not-Being is Being in its true sense. So that we are living in a great obscurity. What we imagine to be real is not real, and yet emanates from the real, for the Real is the Whole. Both Being and Not-Being are accordingly Tao. But above all, never forget that 'Tao' is merely a sound uttered by a human being, and that *the idea is essentially inexpressible.* All things appreciable to the senses, and all cravings of the heart are unreal. Tao is the source of Heaven and Earth. One begat Two, two begat Three, Three begat Millions. And Millions return again into One.

'If you remember this well, young man, you have passed the first gateway on the path of Wisdom.

'You know, then, that Tao is the source of everything: of the trees, the flowers, the birds; of the sea, the desert, and the rocks; of light and darkness; of heat and cold; of day and night; of summer and winter, and of your own life. Worlds and Oceans evaporate in Eternity. Man rises out of the darkness, laughs in the glimmering light, and disappears. But in all these changes the One is manifested. Tao is in everything. Your soul in her innermost is Tao.

'You see the world outspread before you, young man?'

With a stately gesture he pointed seawards.

The hills on either side stood fast, uncompromising, clear-set in the atmosphere—like strong thoughts, petrified, hewn out by conscious energy—yielding only in the distance to the tender influence of light and air. On a very high point stood a lonely little tree, of delicate leafage, in a high light. The evening began to fall with tender serenity; and a rosy glow, dreamy yet brilliant, lent to the mountains, standing ever more sharply-defined against it, an air of peaceful joyousness. In it all was to be felt a gentle upwardstriving, a still poising, as in the rarefied atmosphere of conscious piety. And the sea crept up softly, with a still-swaying slide—with the quiet, irresistible approach of a type of infinity. The sail of a little vessel, gleaming softly golden, glided nearer. So tiny it looked on that immense ocean—so fearless and lovely! All was pure—no trace of foulness was anywhere.

And I spoke with the rare impulse of a mighty joy.

'I feel it now, O Master! That which I seek is everywhere. I had no need to seek it in the distance; for it is quite close to me. It is everywhere—what I seek, what I myself am, what my soul is. It is familiar to me as my own self. It is all revelation! God is everywhere! Tao is in everything!'

'That is so, boy, but confuse it not![4] In that which you see is Tao, but Tao is not what you see. You must not think that Tao is visible to your eyes. Tao will neither waken joy in your heart, nor draw your tears. For all your experiences and emotions are relative and not real.

'However, I will speak no more of that at present. You stand as yet but at the first gate, and see but the first glint of dawn. It is already much that you should realize Tao as present in everything. It will render your life more natural and confident—for, believe me, you lie as safe in the arms of Tao as a child in the arms of its mother. And it will make you serious and thoughtful too, for you will feel yourself to be in all places as holy a thing as is a good priest in his temple. No longer will you be frightened by the changes in things, by life and death; for you know that death, as well as life, emanates from Tao. And it is so natural that Tao, which pervaded your life, should also after death continually surround you.

'Look at the landscape before you! The trees, the mountains, the sea, they are your brothers, like the air and the light. Observe how the sea is approaching us! So spontaneously, so naturally, so purely "because so it must be."—Do you see your dear sister, the little tree on yonder point, bending towards you? And the simple movement of her little leaves?—Then I will speak to you of Wu-Wei,[5] of "non-resistance", of "self-movement" on the breath of your impulse as it was born out of Tao. Men would be true men if they would but let their lives flow of themselves, as the sea heaves, as a flower blooms, in the simple beauty of Tao. In every man there 'is an impulse towards that movement which, proceeding from Tao, would urge him back to Tao again. But men grow blind through their own senses and lusts. They strive for pleasure, desire, hate, fame and riches. Their movements are fierce and stormy, their progress a series of wild uprisings and violent falls. They hold fast to all that is unreal. They desire too many things to allow of their desiring the One. They desire, too, to be wise and good, and that is worst of all. They desire to know too much.

'The one remedy is: the return to the source whence they came. In us is Tao. Tao is rest. Only by renunciation of desire—even the desire for goodness or wisdom—can we attain rest. Oh! all this craving to know what Tao is! And this painful struggle for words in which to express it and to inquire after it!—The truly wise follow the Teaching which is wordless—which remains unexpressed.[6] And who shall ever express it? Those who know it (what Tao is) tell it not; those who tell it, know it not.[7] Even I shall not tell you what Tao is. Yourself must discover it, in that you free yourself from all your passions and cravings, and live in utter spontaneity, void of unnatural striving. Gently must Tao be approached, with a motion reposeful as the movement of that broad ocean. That moves, not because it chooses to move, nor because it knows that it is wise or good to move; it moves involuntarily, unconscious of movement. Thus will you also return to Tao, and when you are returned you will know it not, for you yourself will be Tao.'

He ceased speaking, and looked at me gently. His eyes shone with a quiet light, still and even as the tint of the heavens.

'Father,' I said, 'what you say is beautiful as the sea, and it seems simple as nature; but surely it is not so easy—this strifeless, inactive absorption of man into Tao?'

'Do not confuse words one with another,' he replied. 'By strifelessness—Wu-Wei—Lao-Tse did not mean common inaction,—not mere idling, with closed eyes. He meant: relaxation from earthly activity, from desire—from the craving for unreal things. But he *did* exact activity in *real* things. He implied a powerful movement of the soul, which must be freed from its gloomy body like a bird from its cage. He meant a yielding to the inner motive-force which we derive from Tao, and which leads us to Tao again. And, believe me: this movement is as natural as that of the cloud above us…'

High in the blue ether over our heads were golden clouds, sailing slowly towards the sea. They gleamed with a wonderful purity, as of a high and holy love. Softly, softly they were floating away.

'In a little while they will be gone, vanished in the infinity of the heavens,' said the hermit, 'and you will see nothing but the eternal blue. Thus will your soul be absorbed into Tao.'

'My life is full of sins,' I answered; 'I am heavily burdened with darkening desires. And so are my benighted fellowmen. How can *our* life ever—thus ethereally, in its purest essence—float towards Tao? It is so heavy with evil, it must surely sink back into the mire.'

'Do not believe it, do not believe it!' he exclaimed, smiling in gracious kindliness. 'No man can annihilate Tao, and there shines in each one of us the inextinguishable light of the soul. Do not believe that the evilness of humanity is so great and so mighty. The eternal Tao dwells in all; in murderers and harlots as well as in philosophers and poets. All bear within them an indestructible treasure, and not one is better than another. You cannot love the one in preference to the other; you cannot bless the one and damn the other. They are as alike in essence as two gains of sand on this rock. And not one will be banished out of Tao eternally, for all bear Tao within them. Their sins are illusive, having the vagueness of vapours. Their deeds are a false seeming; and their words pass away like ephemeral dreams. They cannot be "bad", they cannot be "good" either. Irresistibly they are drawn to Tao, as yonder waterdrop to the great sea. It may last longer with some than with others, that is all. And a few centuries—what matter they in the face of Eternity? Poor friend! Has your sin made you so fearful? Have you held your sin to be mightier than Tao? Have you held the sin of men to be mightier than Tao?—You have striven to be good overmuch, and so have seen your own misdoing in a falsely clear light. You have desired overmuch goodness in your fellowmen also, and therefore has their sin unduly troubled you. But all this is a seeming. Tao is neither good nor bad. For Tao is real. Tao alone *is*; and the life of all unreal things is a life of false contrasts and relations, which have no independent existence, and do greatly mislead. So, above all, do not desire to be good, neither call yourself bad. Wu-Wei—unstriving, self-impelled—that must you be. Not bad, not good; not little, and not great; not low and not high. And only then will you in reality *be*, even whilst, in the ordinary sense, you are not. When once you are free from all seeming, from all craving and lusting, then will you move of your own impulse, without so much as knowing that you move; and this, the only true life-principle—this free, untrammelled motion towards Tao—will be light and unconscious as the dissolution of the little cloud above you.'

I experienced a sudden sense of freedom. The feeling was not joy—not happiness. It was rather a gentle sense of expansion—a widening of my mental horizon.

'Father,' I said, 'I thank you! This revelation of Tao lends me already an impulse which, though I cannot explain it, yet seems to bear me gently forward.

'How wonderful is Tao! With all my wisdom, with all my knowledge, I have never felt this before!'

'Crave not thus for wisdom!' said the philosopher. 'Do not desire to know too much—so only shall you grow to know intuitively; for the knowledge acquired by unnatural striving only leads away from Tao. Strive not to know all there is to know concerning the men and things around you, nor—and this more especially—concerning their relations and antagonisms. Above all, seek not happiness too greedily, and be not fearful of unhappiness. For neither of these is real. Joy is not real, nor pain either. Tao would not be Tao, were you able to picture it to yourself as pain, as joy, as happiness or unhappiness; for Tao is One Whole, and in it no discords may exist. Hear, how simply it is expressed by Chuang Tse: "The greatest joy is no joy." And pain too will have vanished for you! You must never believe pain to be a real thing, an essential element of existence. Your pain will one day vanish as the mists vanish from the mountains. For, one day you will realize how natural, how spontaneous are all facts of existence; and all the great problems which have held for you mystery and darkness will become Wu-Wei; quite simple, non-resistent, no longer a source of marvel to you. For everything grows out of Tao, everything is a natural part of the great system developed from a single principle. Then nothing will have the power to trouble you, nor to rejoice you any more. You will laugh no more, neither will you weep.—I see you look up doubtfully, as though you found me too hard, too cold. Nevertheless, when you are somewhat further advanced, you will realize that *this* it means, to be in perfect sympathy with Tao. Then, looking upon "pain", you will know that one day it must disappear, because it is unreal; and looking upon "joy", you will understand that it is but a primitive and shadowy joy, dependent upon time and circumstance, and deriving its apparent existence from contrast with pain. Looking upon a goodly man, you will find it wholly natural that he should be as he is, and will experience a foreshadowing of how much goodlier he will be in that day when he shall no longer represent the "kind" and "good". And upon a murderer you will look with all calmness, with neither special love nor special hate; for he is your fellow in Tao, and all his sin is powerless to annihilate Tao within him. Then, for the first time, when you are Wu-Wei at last—not, in the common human sense, existing—then all will be well with you, and you will glide through your life as quietly and naturally as the great sea before us. Naught will ruffle your peace. Your sleep will be dreamless, and consciousness of self will bring no care.[8] You will see Tao in all things, be one with all existence, and look around on the whole of nature as on something with which you are intimate as with yourself. And passing with calm acceptance through the changes of day and night, summer and winter, life and death, you will one day enter into Tao, where there is no more change, and whence you issued once as pure as you now return.'

'Father, what you say is clear—and compels belief. But life is still so dear to me, and I am afraid of death; I am afraid too lest my friends should die, or my wife, or my child! Death seems to me so black and gloomy—and life is bright—bright with the sun, and the green and flowery earth!'

'That is because you fail as yet to feel the perfect naturalness of death, which is equal in reality, to that of life. You think too much of the insignificant body, and the deep grave in which it must lie; but that is the feeling of a prisoner about to be freed, who is troubled at the thought of leaving the dark cell where he has lived so long. You see death in contrast to life; and both are unreal—both are a changing and a seeming. Your soul does but glide out of a familiar sea into an unfamiliar ocean. That which is real in you, your soul, can never pass away, and this fear is no part of her. You must conquer this fear forever; or, better still, it will happen when you are older, and have lived spontaneously, naturally, following the motions of Tao, that you will, of your own accord, cease to feel it. Neither will you then mourn for those who have gone home before you; with whom you will one day be reunited—not knowing, yourself, that you are reunited to them, because these contrasts will no longer be apparent to you…

'…It came to pass once upon a time that Chuang-Tse's wife died, and the widower was found by Hui-Tse sitting calmly upon the ground, passing the time, as was his wont, in beating upon a gong. When Hui-Tse rallied him upon the seeming indifference of his conduct, Chuang-Tse replied:

'"Thy way of regarding things is unnatural. At first, it is true, I was troubled—I could not be otherwise. But after some pondering I reflected that originally she was not of this life, being not only not-born, but without form altogether; and that into this formlessness no life-germ had as yet penetrated. That nevertheless, as in a sun-warmed furrow, life energy then began to stir; out of life-energy grew form, and form became birth. Today another change has completed itself, and she has died. This resembles the rise and fall of the four seasons: spring, autumn, winter, summer. She sleeps calmly in the Great House. Were I now to weep and wail, it were to act as though the soul of all this had not entered into me—therefore, I do it no more.""[9]

This he told in a simple, unaffected manner that showed how natural it appeared to him. But it was not yet clear to me, and I said:

'I find this wisdom terrible; it almost makes me afraid. Life would seem to me so cold and empty, were I as wise as this.'

'Life *is* cold and empty,' he answered, quietly, but with no trace of contempt in his tone;—'and men are as deceptive as life itself. There is not one who knows himself, not one who knows his fellows; and yet they are all alike. There is, in fact, no such thing as life; it is unreal.'

I could say no more, and stared before me into the twilight. The mountains were sleeping peacefully in the tender, bloom-like shimmer of vague night-mists—lying low, like children, beneath the broad heavens. Below us was an indistinct twinkling of little red lights. From the distance rose a sad monotonous song, the wail of a flute accompanying it. In the depths of the darkness lay the sea in its majesty, and the sound of infinitude swelled far and wide.

Then there arose in me a great sadness, and my eyes filled, as with passionate insistence I asked him:

'And what of friendship, then?—And what of love?'

Art

ART

'What is art?' I asked the hermit.

We were sitting upon the mountain side, in the shadow of an overhanging rock. Before us stretched the sea—one endless gleam of light in the sunshine. Golden sails were driving quietly over it, and white seagulls sweeping in noble curvings lightly, hither and thither, while great, snow-pure clouds came up and sailed by in the blue—majestic in progress, steady and slow.

'It is as natural as the sea, the birds, the clouds,' he answered. 'I do not think you will find this so hard to grasp and feel as Tao. You have only to look around you—earth, clouds, atmosphere, everything will teach it you. Poetry has existed as long as heaven and earth.[10]

'Beauty was born with the heavens and the earth. The sun, the moon, and the red mists of morning and evening illumine each other, and yet—inexhaustible and wonderful as are the changes presented by them— Nature's great phenomena—there exist no pigments, as for garments, to dye them withal. All phenomena of the world bring forth sound when set in motion, and every sound implies some motion which has caused it. The greatest of all sounds are wind and thunder.

ART

'Listen to the mountain stream racing over the rocks! As soon as it is set in motion the sound of it—high or low, short or long—makes itself heard, not actually according to the laws of music, it is true, yet having a certain rhythm and system.

'This is the spontaneous voice of heaven and earth; the voice that is caused by movement.

'Well! In the purest state of the human heart—when the fire of the spirit is at its brightest—then, if it be moved, that too will give forth sound. Is it not a wondrous metamorphosis that out of this a literature should be created?'

'So Poetry is the sound of the heart?'

'You will feel how natural this is. Poetry is to be heard and seen everywhere, for the whole of Nature is one great poet. But just because of its simplicity, is it so strict and unalterable. Where the spring of movement is, there flows the sound of the poem. Any other sound is no poetry. The sound must come quite of itself—Wu—Wei—it cannot be generated by any artifices. There are many—how many!—who by unnatural movement force forth sound; but these are no poets—rather do they resemble apes and parrots. Few indeed are the true poets. From these the verse flows of itself, full of music—powerful as the roaring of the torrent amongst the rocks, as the rolling of thunder in the clouds, soft as the swishing of an evening shower, or the gentle breath of a summer night-breeze. Hark! hark to the sea at our feet! Is it not singing a wondrous song? Is it not a very poem? Is it not pure music? See how the waves sway, in ceaseless mobility—one after the other, one over the other—swinging onward and onward—ever further and further—returning to vanish in music once more! Dost thou hear their rhythmic rushing? Oh! great and simple must a poet be—like the sea! His movement, like that of the sea, is an impulse out of Tao, and in that—tranquil, strifeless, obedient as a child—must he let himself go. Great, great is the sea. Great, great is the poet. But greater—greater—is Tao, that which is not great!'

He was silent, listening to the sea, and I saw how the music of it entered into him.

I had reflected much since hearing his first words concerning Tao. I was fearful lest his great and lofty philosophy should mean death to the artist, and that I also, in giving myself over to this wisdom of his, should become incapable of feeling the inspiration of the poet, and of being any more childishly enraptured at the sight of beauty.

But he himself was standing there in the purest ecstasy, as though he were now looking upon the sea for the first time; and reverently, with shining eyes, he listened to the rush of the waves. 'Is it not beautiful?' he said again, 'Is it not beautiful,—this sound, that came out of Tao the soundless? This light that shone out of Tao the lightless? And the word-music: verse, born of Tao the wordless? Do we not live in an endless mystery—resolving one day into absolute truth!'

I was a long time silent. But its very simplicity was hard for me to grasp. And I asked him doubtfully: 'Can it really be so easy to make and sing poems? It is surely not so easy for us to bring forth verse as for the stream to rush over the rocks? Must we not first practise and train ourselves, and learn to know the verse-forms thoroughly? And is not that voluntary action, rather than involuntary motion?'

My question did not embarrass him, and he answered at once:

'Do not let that perplex you. All depends on whether a man has in him the true spring from which the verse should flow, or not. Has he the pure impulse from Tao within him? Or is his life-motive something less simply beautiful? If he *has* that source in him, he is a poet, if he has it not, he is none. By this time you surely realize that, considered from a high standpoint, all men are really poets; for, as I have told you, there exists in all men the essential, original impulse emanating from and returning to Tao. But rarely do we find this impulse alert and strongly developed—rarely are men endowed with perception of the higher revelations of beauty, through which their bank-bound life-stream flows till lost in boundless eternity. One might express it thus: that ordinary men are like still water in swampy ground, in the midst of poor vegetation; while poets are clear streams, flowing amidst the splendour of luxuriant banks to the endless ocean. But I would rather not speak so much in symbols, for that is not plain enough.

'You would fain know whether a man who *has* the true inspiration of the poet must not nevertheless train himself somewhat in his art, or whether he moves in it entirely of himself, like nature? The latter is without doubt the case! For a young poet, having studied verse-form in all its variety for but a short time, suddenly comes to find these forms so natural as to preclude his inclination for any other. His verse assumes beautiful form involuntarily, simply because other movement would be alien. That is just the difference between the poet and the dilettante: that the poet sings his verse spontaneously, from his own impulse, and afterwards, proving it, finds it to be right in sound—in rhythm—in all its movement; whereas the dilettante, after first marking out for himself a certain verse-form according to the approved pattern of the art-learned, proceeds to project by main force a series of wholly soulless words upon it. The soulful words of the poet flowed of themselves just because they were soulful. And, if we view things in their true light, there do actually exist *no* hard and fast forms for poetry, and absolutely no laws; for a verse which flows spontaneously from its source moves of itself, and is independent of all preconceived human standards! The one law is that there shall be no law.

ART

Perhaps you will find this over-daring, young man! But remember that my demonstrations are taken not from men, but out of Tao, and that I know, moreover, but very few true poets. The man who is simple and pure as Nature is rare indeed. Think you that there are many such in your own land?'

This unexpected question embarrassed me, and I wondered what could be his drift. It was hard to answer, too, so I asked him first another question:

'Great Master, I cannot answer until I hear more from you. *Why does* a poet make a poem?'

That seemed to astonish him mightily, for he repeated it, as though doubting if he had heard aright.

'Why does a poet make a poem?'

'Yes, Master, why?'

Then he laughed outright, and said:

'Why does the sea roar? Why does the bird sing? Do you know that, my son?'

'Because they cannot help it, Father, because they

simply must give their nature vent in that way! It is Wu Wei!'

'Quite so! Well,—and why should it be different with a poet?'

I considered, and my answer came none too readily:

'Yes, but it *may* be different. A poet may sing for the sake of creating or enriching a literature where there is none, or it is in danger of dying out. That has a fine sound, but is no pure motive. Or some poets sing in order to cover themselves with glory, to be famous, to be crowned with shining laurels, and to gain smiles from the fair, bright-eyed maidens strewing flowers on the path before them!'

'You must express yourself with greater exactness,' said the hermit, 'and not desecrate words which thousands hold sacred. For poets who sing for such reasons are no poets at all. A poet sings because he sings. He cannot sing with any given purpose, or he becomes a dilettante.'

'Then, Father, supposing a poet to have sung as simply as a bird, may he afterwards take pleasure in the laurels and the roses? May he jealously hate those who wear the laurels of which he deems himself worthy? Or can he belie his soul's convictions, and call beauty ugly, despising the beauty which he has created? Can he call the beautiful hateful, because the laurels come from unwelcome hands? Can he drape himself in a false garb, and elect to act differently from other men in order to gain prominence through eccentricity? Can he deem himself better than the common run of men? Should he press the common hands which applaud him? May he hate them who deride instead of honouring him? How can you interpret to me all these things? They all appear so strange to me, in comparison with the little bird and the great sea!'

'All these questions, young friend, are an answer to *my* question,' he replied; 'for the fact that you would know all this is a proof that there are not many poets in your country. Remember that I understand and use the word "poet" in its purest, highest meaning. A poet can only live for his art, which he loves for itself, and not as a means for securing fleeting earthly pleasures. A poet looks upon men and things—in their nature and relationship—so simply, that he himself approaches very nearly to the nature of Tao. Other men see men and things hazily, as through a fog. The poet realizes this to be an incontestable fact. How then can he expect his simplicity to be understood by this hazy mind of the public? How can he cherish feelings of hate and grief when it ridicules him? How feel pleasure when it would do him honour? It is the same in this case as with the four "seasons" of Chuang-Tse. There is nothing specially agitating in it all, because it is the natural course of things. Consequently the poet is neither in despair when he is not heard, nor happy when he is fêted. He looks upon the state of things with regard to the multitude and the way it comports itself towards him as a natural consequence, of which he knows the cause. The judgment of the common people is not even so much as indifferent to him—it simply does not exist for him. He does not sing his verses for the sake of the people, but because he cannot help himself. The sound of human comment on his work escapes him entirely, and he knows not whether he be famous or forgotten. "The highest fame is no fame."* You look at me, young man, as though I were telling stranger things than you have ever dared to dream. But I am telling nothing but the plainest truth, simple and natural as the truth in landscape or sea. Having dwelt until so lately mid the strenuous life of your countrymen, you have never yet seen true simplicity. For so long you have heard nothing spoken of but "fame", "earnings", "honour", "artists" and "immortality", that, for all you know, these things

---

*From the 'Nan Hwa King', chap. xviii.

may be indispensable as air, and veritable as your soul. But it is all a seeming and deception. Those whom you have seen may indeed have been poets of true fibre, but they had been led astray from the impulse derived from Tao which was their life-principle, and they did not remain what they were, but sank through their weakness to the nature of commonplace men. So that they have come to do as ordinary men do, only they do it more strongly. So much do I gather from your questioning. But all these are poets no longer, and will sing no more true poetry so long as they remain as they are. For the smallest deviation from the original impulse is sufficient to kill the poetry within them. There is but the one direct way: single and simple as a maiden—uncompromising as a straight line. This straight line is spontaneity; on either side of it lie false activity and the unnatural—also the roads to fame and notoriety—where occur murder, and sudden death, and where one bosom friend will suck the lifeblood from another to further the attainment of his own ends. The straight line cuts its own way, without deviation or secret windings, in simple continuance into infinity.

'You understand then, that thus, by the nature of things, all those situations which would convert the poet into the sacrificial victim of the mob become impossible. You have probably read, in the history alike of your country and my own, of poets who have died of grief at want of recognition, or who have taken their own lives on account of undeserved contumely. I have indeed always felt the pathos of this, yet have realized that to such poets as these, the term truly great cannot be applied.

'And I am speaking, of course, not of the artists of speech only, but of all artists. Shall I now show you something by an artist as true and simple-minded as I can conceive a man to be? Come with me then!'

He led me into a small chamber in his hut a cell with white walls and no furniture save a bed, a table covered with books, and a few chairs. He opened a door in the wall, and drew out from it a wooden chest. This he carried as carefully as though it had been some sacred object or a little child. He set it gently down upon the floor, opened the lid, and lifted out a closed shrine of red-brown wood, which he placed upon the table.[11] 'See,' he remarked, 'this is a beautiful shrine, to begin with. A beautiful thing must have a beautiful setting. At present the little doors are shut. Do you not find this a goodly idea: to be able even thus to hold it hidden from profane eyes?—But before *you* I may well open it.'

And the two wings of the shrine flew apart.

Against a background of pale blue silk appeared a large figure, gleaming and shimmering and diffusing a wonderful radiance of its own. It was the Buddha Kwan Yin, seated upon a lotus that reared itself, straight and graceful, and modestly opened, above a tumult of wild waves.[12]

'Do you perceive the utter simplicity and beauty of this?' he asked me; and in his voice there spoke a great and tender love. 'Is not this the very embodiment of perfect rest? How serene is the countenance—how wonderfully tender, and yet how tensely grave, with its closed eyes gazing into infinity!—See—the cheek,—how delicate and tender! See the mouth—and the lofty curving of the eyebrows—and the pure pearl gleaming above her forehead[13]—symbol of a soul taking its flight from the body! And the body—how few are the lines of it! Yet see: what infinite love and mercifulness in the downward pose of the left arm; and in the uplifted right arm—with two raised fingers held together as in the act of preaching—what an indescribable holiness! And how beautiful the repose of the crossed legs resting so softly upon the lotus! And see how tenderly felt—notwithstanding the immense strength and restraint of the whole—the delicate soles of the feet, curved with such subtle gentleness! Is it not the quintessence of the whole of Buddhism in a single picture? You need not to have read anything of Buddhism in order to appreciate it now, here, in all its inmost meaning. Rest—is it not absolute rest—this ideally pure countenance gazing thus stilly into eternity? Love—is it not absolute love for the world—this simple drooping of the arm? And is not the essence of the whole doctrine grasped and confined in the pose of the uplifted fingers?

'And then, the material of which such a figure as this is made! Do you realize, I wonder, that an artist such as this must have laboured for years and years before his material became as pure and ethereal as he required it to be? For the nature of stone is so hard—is it not? And the general idea of it—matter that would suit but ill for the plastic representation of the ideal conception: Rest. So the artist wrought upon all kinds of common materials such as clay, sand and earth, and transformed them by means of fit and harmonious combination with precious stones, pearls and jasper, into costly substances. And so the material for this figure became something that was no longer material, but rather the incarnation of a sublime idea. The artist wished to symbolize also in his representation the rosy dawn which broke upon mankind on the appearance of Buddha; and so, shimmering through the snowy white of his porcelain, he introduced just such a vague rosy glow as plays upon the morning clouds before the glory of the sun bursts forth. Is not this half-realized, growing light more instinct with feeling than light itself? Can you perceive this most indefinite, yet clear and rosy colour shimmering throughout the white? Is it not chaste as the first soft blush of a maiden? Is it not the godly love of the artist which thus glows in the pureness of the white? Such a figure is, in fact, no longer a figure. The idea of material is entirely obliterated; it is an inspiration.'

For a long time I was too much moved to speak. More strongly yet than the pure wisdom of the old man, did the beauty of this art take hold upon and purify my soul. At last I asked gently:

'Who has created this marvel? I would fain know, that I may hold his name with yours in veneration.'

'That is of little importance, my young friend!' he answered. 'The soul that was in this artist is absorbed again into Tao, just as yours will be one day. His body has fallen away, like the leaves from a tree, just as yours in time will fall away. What weight can attach then to his name? Nevertheless, I will tell it to you; he was called Tan Wei,[14] and he engraved this name in finely-devised characters upon the back of the figure, such being the custom at that time. Who was he? A common workman, surely, who did not even know, himself, that he was an artist; who seemed to himself nothing more than a common peasant, and who had not the least suspicion that his work was so beautiful. But he must have gazed much at the heavens and clouds above him, and loved the wide seas, and the landscapes, and the flowers; otherwise he could not have been so fine in feeling; for such simple lines and pure colours are only to be found in Nature. He was certainly not celebrated; you will not find his name in any history. I could not tell you whence he came, how he lived, or to what age. I know only that it is more than four hundred years since such figures as these were made, and that connoisseurs reckon that this one dates from the first half of the Ming Dynasty. Most probably the artist lived quite quietly the same sort of life as the other people, worked industriously as a common labourer, and died humbly, unconscious of his own greatness. But his work remained, and this image, which by a fortunate chance has found its way to this district, where the last wars never raged, which is still the same as when he made it. And thus it may last on for centuries and centuries, in inextinguishable radiance, in maidenly majesty. O, to create such a thing, in pure, unconscious simplicity—that is to be a poet! That is the art which dates not from time but from eternity! How beautiful it is! Do you not find it so too? This porcelain that is almost indestructible; this radiance, which never dies away! Here upon the earth it stands, so strong and yet so tender, and so it will still be, long after our successors are dead!—And the soul of the artist is with Tao!'

We continued long to look upon the image. Then he took careful hold of the shrine once more.

'It is so delicate,' he said, 'that I hardly dare to expose it to broad daylight. For this miracle of tenderness—ethereal as a soul—the daylight is too hard. I feel a kind of anxiety lest the light should suddenly break it in pieces; or cause it to dissolve like a little light cloud—so wholly soul-like is its composition!'

And softly, very softly, he replaced the shrine within the chest, which he closed.

He went out now, before me, and we seated ourselves again beneath the overhanging rock.

'How beautiful it would be,' I said, 'if everyone could make things like that, in all simplicity, and surround themselves with them, everywhere!'

'Every one!' he answered; 'well, that is perhaps too much to expect! But there really was once a time when this great kingdom was one great temple of art and beauty. You may still see the traces of it here in China. At that time the greater number of the people were simple-minded artists. All objects surrounding them were beautiful, the smallest thing as well as the greatest—whether it were a temple, a garden, a table, a chair, or a knife. Just examine the little tea-cups, or the smallest censers of that period!

The poorest coolie ate out of vessels as perfect in their way as my Kwan-Yin image. All objects were beautifully made, and involuntarily so. The simple artisans did not consider themselves "artists", or in any way different from their fellow-men, and no petty strife can have arisen between them, otherwise there would have been an end of their art. Everything was beautiful because they were all single-minded and worked honestly. It was as natural in those days for things to be beautiful as it is nowadays for them to be ugly. The art of China has sunk to its lowest ebb; that is a consequence of its miserable social condition. You have surely remarked that the art of the country is deteriorating. And that is a death-sign for this great Empire. For Art is inseparably connected with the full-bloom of a country's life. If the art declines, then the whole country degenerates. I do not mean this in the political, but rather in the moral sense. For a morally-strong and simple-hearted people brings forth involuntarily a strong and healthy art. Yes, what you said is true; how much better would men's lives be, could they but create for themselves better surroundings! And how extraordinary that this is not done! For Nature remains ever and everywhere accessible to them. See the clouds—the trees—the sea!'

The sea was still as ever, splashing at our feet—boundless and pure. Clouds sailed majestically landwards, with a slow motion, in the full blaze of the light. Golden gleams, falling upon the mountains, vanished again with the rhythmical sweep of the clouds. Light and motion, sound and play of colour, everywhere!

The hermit gazed calmly and confidingly at this infinite loveliness; as though deeply conscious of the intimate relationship existing between him and all his surroundings. He seemed to guess what was in my mind as I looked at him, for he said:

'We fit as naturally into this beauty around us as a tree or a mountain. If we can but remain so always, we shall retain the feeling of our own well-being amid all the great workings of the world-system. So much has been said about human life; and scholars have created such an endless labyrinth of theories! And yet in its inmost kernel it is as plain as Nature. All things are equal in simplicity, and nothing is really in confusion, however much it may seem as though it were so. Everything moves surely and inevitably as the sea.'

There rang in his voice both the great love of the poet and the quiet assurance of the scholar who takes his stand upon incontrovertible truth.

'Are you satisfied for today?' was his friendly question; 'and have I helped you forward a little? Do you feel more clearly what poetry is?'

'Father,' I answered, your wisdom is poetry, and your poetry is wisdom! How can that be?

'That is quite true, from your point of view,' he answered. 'But you have yet to learn that all these words are but a seeming. I know not what my wisdom is, nor my poetry. It is all one. It is so simple and natural when you understand this! It is all Tao.'

LOVE

LOVE

Once more it was evening. We sat again upon the soft turf of the mountain-side, the quietness of our mood in sympathy with the solemn stillness of twilight. The distant mountain ranges reposed in an atmosphere breathing reverence and devotion—they seemed to be kneeling beneath the heavens, beneath the slow-descending blessing of night. The isolated trees dotted here and there about the hills stood motionless, in a pause of silent worshipping. The rush of the sea sounded distant and indistinct, lost in its own greatness. Peace lay over everything, and soft sounds went up, as of prayer.

The hermit stood before me, dignified as a tree in the midst of Nature, and awe-inspiring as the evening itself.

I had returned to question him again. For my soul found no repose apart from him, and a mighty impulse was stirring within me. But now that I found myself near him, I hardly dared to speak; and indeed it seemed as though words were no longer necessary—as though everything lay, of itself, open and clear as daylight. How goodly and simple everything appeared that evening! Was it not my own inmost being that I recognized in all the beauty around me? And was not the whole on the point of being absorbed into the Eternal?

Nevertheless I broke in upon this train of feeling, and cleft the peaceful silence with my voice:

'Father,' I said sadly, 'all your words have sunk into my mind, and my soul is filled with the balm of them. This soul of mine is no longer my own—no longer what I used to be. It is as though I were dead: and I know not what is taking place within me—by day and by night—causing it to grow so light, and clear, and vacant in my mind. Father, I know it is Tao; it is death, and glorious resurrection; but it is not love; and without love, Tao appears to me but a gloomy lie.'

The old man looked round him at the evening scene, and smiled gently.

'What is love?' he asked calmly. 'Are you sure about that, I wonder?'

'No, I am not sure,' I answered. 'I do not know

anything about it, but that is just the reason of its great blessedness. Yes, do but let me express it! I mean love of a maiden, love of a woman. I remember yet, Father, what it was to me when I saw the maiden, and my soul knew delight for the first time. It was like a sea, like a broad heaven, like death. It was light—and I had been blind! It hurt, Father—my heart beat so violently—and my eyes burned. The world was a fire, and all things were strange, and began to live. It was a great flame flaring from out my soul. It was so fearful, but so lovely, and so infinitely great! Father, I think it was greater than Tao!'

'I know well what it was,' said the sage. 'It was Beauty, the earthly form of the formless Tao, calling up in you the rhythm of that movement by which you will enter into Tao. You might have experienced the same at the sight of a tree, a cloud, a flower. But because you are human, living by desire, therefore to you it could only be revealed through another

LOVE

human being, a woman—because, also, that form is to you more easily understood, and more familiar. And since desire did not allow the full upgrowth of a pure contemplation, therefore was the rhythm within you wrought up to be wild tempest, like a storm-thrashed sea that knows not whither it is tending. The inmost essence of the whole emotion was not "love", but Tao.'

But the calmness of the old sage made me impatient, and excited me to answer roughly:

'It is easy to talk thus theoretically, but seeing that you have never experienced it yourself, you can understand nothing of that of which you speak!'

He looked at me steadily, and laid his hand sympathetically on my shoulder.

'It would be cruel of you to speak thus to any one but me, young man! I loved, before you drew breath in this world! At that time there lived a maiden, so wondrous to see, it was as if she were the direct-born expression of Tao. For me she was the world, and the world lay dead around her. I saw nothing but her, and for me there existed no such things as trees, men, or clouds. She was more beautiful than this evening, gentler than the lines of those distant mountains, more tender than those hushed tree-tops; and the light of her presence was more blessed to see than the still shining of yonder star. I will not tell you her story. It was more scorching than a very hell-fire—but it was not real, and it is over now, like a storm that has passed. It seemed to me that I must die; I longed to flee from my pain into death. But there came a dawning in my soul, and all grew light and comprehensible. Nothing was lost. All was yet as it had been. The beauty which I believed to have been taken from me lived on still, spotless, in myself. For not from this woman—out of my soul had this beauty sprung; and this I saw shining yet, all over the world, with an everlasting radiance, Nature was no other than what I had fashioned to myself out of that shadowy form of a woman. And my soul was one with Nature, and floated with a like rhythm towards the eternal Tao.'

Calmed by his calmness, I said: 'She whom *I* loved is dead, Father. She who culled my soul as a child culls a flower, never became my wife. But I have a wife now, a miracle of strength and goodness, a wife who is essential to me as light and air. I do not love her as I even now love the dead. But I know that she is a purer human being than that other. How is it then that I do *not* love her so much? She has transformed my wild and troubled life into a tranquil march towards death. She is simple and true as Nature itself, and her face is dear to me as the sunlight.'

'You love her, indeed!' said the sage, 'but you know not what love means, nor loving. I will tell it you. Love is no other than the rhythm of Tao. I have told you: you are come out of Tao, and to Tao you will return. Whilst you are young—with your soul still enveloped in darkness—in the shock of the first impulse within you, you know not yet whither you are trending. You see the woman before you. You believe her to be that towards which the rhythm is driving you. But even when the woman is yours, and you have thrilled at the touch of her, you feel the rhythm yet within you, unappeased, and know that you must forward, ever further, if you would bring it to a standstill. Then it is that in the soul of the man and of the woman there arises a great sadness, and they look at one another, questioning whether they are now bound. Gently they clasp one another by the hand, and move on through life, swayed by the same impulse, towards the same goal. Call this love if you will. What is a name? I call it Tao. And the souls of those who love are like two white clouds floating softly side by side, that vanish, wafted by the same wind, into the infinite blue of the heavens.'

'But that is not the love that I mean!' I cried.

LOVE

'Love is not the desire to see the loved one absorbed into Tao; love is the longing to be always with her; the deep yearning for the blending of the two souls in one; the hot desire to soar, in one breath with her, into felicity! And this always with the loved one alone—not with others, not with Nature. And were I absorbed into Tao, all this happiness would be forever lost! Oh let me stay here, in this goodly world, with my faithful companion! Here it is so bright and homely, and Tao is still so gloomy and inscrutable for me.'

'The hot desire dies out,' he answered calmly. 'The body of your loved one will wither and pass away within the cold earth. The leaves of the trees fade in autumn, and the withered flowers droop sadly to the ground. How can you love that so much which does not last? However, you know in truth, as yet, neither how you love, nor what it is that you love. The beauty of woman is but a vague reflection of the formless beauty of Tao. The emotion it awakens, the longing to lose yourself in her beauty, that ecstasy of feeling which would lend wings for the flight of your soul with the beloved—beyond horizon-bounds, into regions of bliss—believe me, it is no other than the rhythm of Tao; only you know it not. You resemble still the river which knows as yet only its shimmering banks; which has no knowledge of the power that draws it forward; but which will one day inevitably flow out into the great ocean. Why this striving after happiness, after human happiness, that lasts but a moment and then vanishes again? Chuang-Tse said truly: "The highest happiness is no happiness." Is it not small and pitiable—this momentary uprising, and down-falling, and uprising again? This wavering, weakly intention and progress of men? Do not seek happiness in a woman. She is the joyful revelation of Tao directed towards you. She is the purest form in the whole of Nature by which Tao is manifested. She is the gentle force that awakens the rhythm of

LOVE

Tao within you. But she is only a poor creature like yourself. And you are for her the same joyful revelation that she is to you. Fancy not that that which you perceive in her is that Tao, that very holiest, into which you would one day ascend! For then you would surely reject her when you realized what she was. If you will truly love a woman, then love her as being of the same poor nature as yourself, and do not seek happiness with her. Whether in your love you see this or not—her inmost being is Tao. A poet looks upon a woman, and, swayed by the 'rhythm,' he perceives the beauty of the beloved in all things—in the trees, the mountains, the horizon; for the beauty of a woman is the same as that of Nature. It is the form of Tao, the great and formless, and what your soul desires in the excitement of beholding—this strange, unspeakable feeling—is nothing but your oneness with this beauty, and with the source of this beauty—Tao. And the like is experienced by your wife. You are for each other angels, who lead one another to Tao unconsciously.'

I was silent for a while, reflecting. In the soft colouring and stillness of the evening lay a great sadness. Above the horizon, where the sun had set, there glimmered a streak of faint red light, like dying pain.

'What is this sadness, then, in the Nature around us?' I asked. 'Is there not that in the twilight as though the whole earth were weeping with a grievous longing? See how she mourns, with these fading hues, these drooping tree-tops, and solemn mountains. Human eyes must fill with tears, when this great grief of Nature looms within their sight. It is as though she were longing for her beloved—as though everything—seas, mountains and heavens—were full of mourning.'

And the Sage replied: 'It is the same pain which cries in the hearts of men. Your own longing quivers in Nature too. The "Heimweh" of the evening is also the "Heimweh" of your soul. Your soul has lost her love: Tao, with whom she once was one; and your soul desires re-union with her love. Absolute re-union with Tao—is not that an immense love?—To be so absolutely one with the beloved that you are wholly hers, she wholly yours;—a union so full and eternal that neither death nor life can ever cleave your oneness again? So tranquil and pure that desire can no more awaken in you—perfect blessedness being attained, and a holy and permanent peace? For Tao is one single, eternal, pure infinitude of soul.

'Is that not more perfect than the love of a woman? This poor, sad love, each day of which reveals to you some sullying of the clear life of the soul by dark and sanguine passion? When you are absorbed into Tao, then only will you be completely, eternally united with the soul of your beloved, with the souls of all men, your brothers, and with the soul of Nature. And the few moments of blessedness fleetingly enjoyed by all lovers upon earth are as nothing in comparison with that endless bliss: the blending of the souls of all who love in an eternity of perfect purity.'

A horizon of blessedness opened out before my soul, wider than the vague horizon of the—sea, wider than the heavens.

'Father!' I cried in ecstasy, 'can it be that everything is so holy, and I have never known it? I have been so filled with longing, and so worn out with weeping; and my breast has been heavy with sobs and dread. I have been so consumed with fear! I have trembled at the thought of death! I have despaired of all things being good when I saw so much suffering around me. I have believed myself damned, by reason of the wild passions, the bodily desires, burning within and flaming without me—passions which, though hating them, I still was, coward-like, condemned to serve. With what breathless horror I have realized how the tender, flower-like body of my love must one day moulder and crumble away in the cold, dark earth! I have believed that I should never feel again that blessed peace at the look in her eyes, through which her soul was shining. And was it Tao! Was Tao really even then always within me, like a faithful guardian? And was it Tao that shone from her eyes? Was Tao in everything that surrounded me—in the clouds, the trees and the sea? Is the inmost being of earth and heaven, then, also the inmost being of my beloved and my own soul? Is it *that* for which there burns within me that mysterious longing which I did not understand, and which drove me so restlessly onward? I thought it was leading me away from the beloved, and that I was ceasing to love her! Was it really the rhythm of Tao, then, that moved my beloved too? The same as that in which all Nature breathes, and all suns and planets pursue their shining course throughout eternity?—Then all is indeed made holy! Then Tao is indeed in everything, as my soul is in Tao! Oh, Father, Father! it is growing so light in my heart! My soul seems to foresee that which will come one day;

and the heavens above us, and the great sea, they foretell it too! See, how reverent is the pose of these trees around us—and see the lines of the mountains, how soft in their holy repose! All Nature is filled with sacred awe, and my soul too thrills with ecstasy, for she has looked upon her beloved!'

I sat there long, in silent, still, forgetfulness. It was to me as though I were one with the soul of my master and with Nature. I saw nothing and heard nothing;—void of all desire, bereft of all will, I lay sunk in the deepest peace. I was awakened by a soft sound close by me. A fruit had fallen from the tree to the ground behind us. When I looked up, it was into shimmering moonlight. The recluse was standing by me, and bent over me kindly.

'You have strained your spirit overmuch, my young friend!' he said concernedly. 'It is too much for you in so short a time. You have fallen asleep from exhaustion. The sea sleeps too. See, not a furrow breaks its even surface; motionless, dreaming, it receives the benediction of the light. But, you must awaken! It is late, your boat is ready, and your wife awaits you at home in the town.'

I answered, still half dreaming: 'I would so gladly stay here! Let me return, with my wife, and stay here for ever! I cannot go back to the people again! Ah, Father, I shudder—I can see their scoffing faces, their insulting glances, their disbelief, and their irreverence! How can I retain the wondrous light and tender feeling of my soul in the midst of that ungracious people? How can I ever so hide it under smile or speech that they shall never detect it, nor desecrate it with their insolent ridicule?'

Then, laying his hand earnestly upon my shoulder, he said:

'Listen carefully to what I now say to you, my friend, and above all, *believe* me. I shall give you pain, but I cannot help it. You *must* return to the world and your fellowmen; it cannot be otherwise. You have spoken too much with me already; perhaps I have said somewhat too much to you. Your further growth must be your own doing, and you must find out everything for yourself. Be only simple of heart, and you will discover everything without effort, like a child finding flowers. At this moment you feel deeply and purely, what I have said to you. This present mood is one of the highest moments of your life. But you cannot yet be strong enough to maintain it. You will relapse, and spiritual feeling will turn again to words and theories. Only by slow degrees will you grow once more to feel it purely and keep it permanently. When that is so, then you may return hither in peace, and then you will do well to remain here;—but by that time I shall be long dead.

'You must complete your growth in the midst of life, not outside it; for you are not yet pure enough to rise above it. A moment ago, it is true, you were

LOVE

equal even to that, but the reaction will soon set in. You may not shun the rest of mankind; they are your equals, even though they may not feel so purely as you do. You can go amongst them as their comrade, and take them by the hand; only do not let them look upon your soul, so long as they are still so far behind you. They would not mock you from evil-mindedness, but rather out of religious persuasion, being unaware how utterly miserable, how godless, how forsaken they are, and how far from all those holy things by which you actually live. You must be so strong in your conviction that nothing can hinder you. And that you will only become after a long and bitter struggle. But out of your tears will grow your strength, and through pain you will attain peace. Above all remember that Tao, Poetry and Love are one and the same, although you may seek to define it by these several vague terms;—that it is always within you and around you;—that it never forsakes you; and that you are safe and well cared for in this holy environment. You are surrounded with benefits, and sheltered by a love which is eternal. Everything is rendered holy through the primal force of Tao dwelling within it.'

He spoke so gently and convincingly that I had no answer to give. Willingly I allowed myself to be guided by him to the shore. My boat lay motionless upon the smooth water, awaiting me.

'Farewell, my young friend! Farewell!' he said, calmly and tenderly. 'Remember all that I have told you!'

But I could not leave him in such a manner. Suddenly I thought of the loneliness of his life in this place, and tears of sympathy rose to my eyes. I grasped his hand.

'Father, come with me!' I besought him. 'My wife and I will care for you; we will do everything for you; and when you are sick we will tend you. Do not stay here in this loneliness, so void of all the love that might make life sweet to you!'

He smiled gently, and shook his head as a father might at some fancy of his child's, answering with tranquil kindness:

'You have lapsed already! Do you realize now how necessary it is for you to remain in the midst of the everyday life? I have but this moment told you how great is the love which surrounds me—and still you deem me lonely here and forsaken? Here, in Tao, I am as safe at home as a child is with its mother. You mean it well, my friend, but you must grow wiser, much wiser! Be not concerned for me; that is unnecessary, grateful though I am to you for this feeling. Think of yourself just now. And do what I say. Believe that I tell you that which is best for you. In the boat lies something which should remind you of the days you have spent here. Farewell!'

I bent silently over his hand and kissed it. I thought I felt that it trembled with emotion; but when I looked at him again his face was calm and cheerful as the moon in the sky.

I stepped into the boat, and the boatman took up the oars. With dextrous strokes he drove it over the even surface of the water. I was already some way from the land when my foot struck against some object in the boat, and I remembered that something for me was lying there. I took it up. It was a small chest. Hastily I lifted the lid. And in the soft, calm moonlight there gleamed with mystical radiance the wonderful porcelain of the Kwan-Yin image, the same which the old man had cherished so carefully, and loved so well.

There, in the lofty tranquility of severe yet gentle lines, in all the ethereal delicacy of the transparent porcelain, reposed the pure figure of Kwan-Yin, shining as with spiritual radiance amidst the shimmering petals of the lotus.

I scarcely dared believe that this holy thing had been given to me. I seized my handkerchief, and waved with it towards the shore, to convey to the recluse my thanks. He stood there motionless, gazing straight before him. I waited longingly for him to wave—for one more greeting from him—one more sign of love—but he remained immovable.

Was it I after whom he was gazing? Was he gazing at the sea?...

I closed the lid of the chest, and kept it near me, as though it had been a love of his which I was bearing away. I knew now that he cared for me; but his imperturbable serenity was too great for me—it saddened my mood that he had never signed to me again.

We drew further and further away; the outlines of his figure grew fainter and fainter; at last I could see it no more.

He remained; with the dreams of his soul, in the midst of Nature—alone in infinity—bereft of all human love—but close to the great bosom of Tao.

I took my way back to the life amongst mankind, my brothers and equals—in all the souls of whom dwells Tao, primordial and eternal.

The ornamental lights of the harbour gleamed already in the distance, and the drone of the great town sounded nearer and nearer to us over the sea.

Then I felt a great strength in me, and I ordered the boatman to row still more quickly. I was ready. Was I not as safely and well cared for in the great town as in the still country?—In the street as on the sea?

In everything, everywhere, dwells Poetry—Love—Tao. And the whole world is a great sanctuary, well-devised and surely-maintained as a strong, well-ordered house.

NOTES

1. **p. 5.** This is a fact. Chinese priests are in the habit of repeating Sutras which, to judge by the sound, have been translated from the Sanskrit into Chinese phrases of which they do not understand one word.
2. **p. 8.** The 'Yellow Emperor' is a legendary emperor,

who appears to have reigned about the year 2697 B.C.

3. **p. 8.** That which follows in inverted commas is an extract translated from the twelfth chapter of the 'Nan Hwa King.'

4. **p. 14.** The following passage, as far as the sentence 'and the Millions return again into One' is an adaptation—not a translation—of the first section of 'Tao-Teh-King.' Lao-Tse's wonderfully simple writing cannot possibly be translated into equally simple passages in our language. This rendering of mine—arrived at partly by aid of Chinese commentators—is an entirely new reading, and is, to the best of my knowledge, the true one. One of the most celebrated, and, in a certain sense, one of the most competent of the sinologues, Herbert Giles, translates of this first section only the first sentence, and finds the rest not worth the trouble of translating! (compare 'The Remains of Lao Tzŭ,' by H. A. Giles, Honkong, *China Mail* Office, 1886).

This same scholar translates 'Tao' as 'the Way', not

NOTES

perceiving how impossible it is that which Lao-Tse meant—the highest of all, the infinite—should be a 'way,' seeing that a way (in the figurative sense) always leads to something else, and therefore cannot be the highest. Another still more celebrated sinologue, Dr. Legge, translates 'Tao' as 'Course', and out of the simple sentence: 'If Tao could be expressed in words it would not be the eternal Tao' he makes: 'The Course that can be trodden is not the enduring and unchanging course.' The whole secret is this: that the sign or word 'Tao' has a great number of meanings, and that in Confucius's work 'Chung Yung' it does as a matter of fact mean 'Way'; but in a hundred other instances it means: 'speech, expression, a saying.' Lao-Tse having, in one sentence, used this sign in two different senses, nearly all translators have suffered themselves to be misled. The sentence is as simple as possible, and in two of my Chinese editions the commentators put: 'spoken,' and: 'by word of mouth.' But of all the sinologues only Wells Williams has translated this sentence well, namely thus: 'The Tao which can be expressed is not the eternal Tao.' Although the construction of the phrase is not accurately rendered, at any rate Williams has grasped the meaning.

After my work had already appeared in the periodical *De Gids,* I saw for the first time Professor de Groot's work 'Jaarlijksche feesten en gebruiken der Emoy Chineezen,' from which I gathered that he agreed with me in so far as to say also that 'Tao' was untranslatable—a sub-lying conception 'for which the Chinese philosopher himself could find no name, and which he consequently stamped with the word 'Tao.' Professor de Groot adds: 'If one translates this word by 'the universal soul of Nature,' 'the all-pervading energy of nature,' or merely by the word 'Nature' itself, one will surely not be far from the philosopher's meaning."

Although the term holds for me something still higher, yet I find Professor de Groot's conception of it the most sympathetic of all those known to me.

5.   **p. 15.** This 'Wu-Wei'—untranslatable as it is in

NOTES

fact—has been rendered by these sinologues into *'inaction'*—as though it signified idleness, inertia. It most certainly does not signify idleness, however, but rather *action,* activity—that is to say: 'inactivity of the perverted, unnatural passions and desires,' but 'activity in the sense of natural movement proceeding from Tao.' Thus, in the 'Nan Hwa King' we find the following: 'The heavens and the earth do nothing' (in the evil sense) 'and' (yet) 'there is nothing which they do not do.' The whole of nature consists in 'Wu-Wei,' in natural, from-Tao-emanating movement. By translating Wu-Wei into 'inaction' the sinologues have arrived at the exact opposite of the meaning of the Chinese text.

Lao-Tse himself does not dilate further upon the subject. What follows here is my own conception of the text. The whole first chapter of the original occupies only one page in the book, and contains only fifty-nine characters. It testifies to Lao-Tse's wonderful subtlety and terseness of language that he was able in so few words to say so much.

6. **p. 16.** This sentence is translated from the 'Tao-Teh-King' (Chapter ii)

7. **p. 16.** From the 56th chapter. This sentence is also to be found in 15th chapter of the 'Nan Hwa King'.

8. **p. 24.** This runs somewhat as follows in the 6th chapter of the Nan Hwa King: 'The true men of the early ages slept dreamlessly, and were conscious of self without care.'

9. **p. 27.** This episode is translated from the 18th section of the 'Nan Hwa King'. By the 'Great House' Chuang-Tse meant, of course, the universe, and this expression 'house' lends to the passage a touch of familiar intimacy, showing Chuang-Tse to have the feeling that the dead one was well cared-for, as though within the shelter of a house.— H. Giles, who renders it 'Eternity', which does not appear at all in the Chinese text, loses by his translation the confiding element which makes Chuang-Tse's speech so touching. (Compare 'Chuang Tsy', by H. Giles, London, Bernard Quaritch, 1889). The actual words are: 'Ku Shih' = Great House.

NOTES

10. **p. 32.** The following, to the end of the sentence: 'Poetry is the sound of the heart,' has been translated by me from a preface by Ong Giao Ki to his edition of the Poetry of the Tang-Dynasty. Ong Giao Ki lived in the first half of the eighteenth century.

11. **p. 46.** The Chinese do really preserve their treasures in this careful manner. It is usual for an antique figure of Buddha to lie in a silk-lined shrine, the shrine in a wooden chest, and the chest in a cloth. It is unpacked upon great occasions.

12. **p. 47.** Such a figure as the above-described is not a mere figment of the author's imagination—such figures really exist. A similar one is in the possession of the author.

13. **p. 47.** The soul-pearl 'Durma'.

14. **p. 50.** The figure in the author's possession is by Tan Wei. Another great artist was Ho Chao Tsung, of certain figures by whom I have also, with very great trouble, become possessed of. These names are well known to every artist, but I have endeavoured in vain to discover anything nearer with regard to them. They became famous after death; but they had lived in such simplicity and oblivion, that now not even their birthplace is remembered. One hears conjectures, but I could arrive at no certainty.